Killer WHALES

Text Vicki León

Photographs Jeff Foott

Design Ashala Nicols-Lawler

ISBN 1 85648 017 8

This edition published by
The Promotional Reprint Company Limited for
Bookmart Limited (Registered No. 2372865)
Desford Road, Enderby, Leicester, U.K.

Printed and bound in Hong Kong

The mysterious and beautiful life of the orca

"KILLER" seems like an odd name for such an elegant animal. Outfitted with smooth black-and-white skin that resembles a well-tailored tuxedo, the killer whale looks too well-mannered, too toylike, to be the top predator of the sea. Especially when you learn that *Orcinus orca* is, biologically speaking, an overgrown dolphin. Today the trend is to call these graceful creatures "orcas."

Orcas and dolphins are *Odontoceti* or toothed whales and members of the same Delphinid family. Dolphins average ten feet in length; orcas can be twice that length or more.

I had seen captive orcas in California and Hawaii, but it wasn't until I saw them in a Canadian underwater display that I grasped just how big they are. At the Vancouver Aquarium, you see a vast, bedroom-sized animal that glides and turns as sharply as any aquarium fish, skimming easily under the colossal bodies of other killer whales. At this and other oceanaria, you can press your own puny body up against the glass for comparison purposes. When the orcas feel like it, the window on their side becomes wall-to-wall whale.

Killer whales come equipped with all the tools necessary to be the supreme hunting machines in the sea. Four to ten tons of muscular power. A cruising speed that can hit 30 miles an hour. An appetite which requires more than 100+ pounds of animal protein daily. And an intelligence and fearlessness that make them more than a match for any creature in the ocean and a few on land as well.

The orca also possesses 46 to 50 cone-shaped teeth that interlock, forming a tight curtain of ivory from which there is no escape. Killer whales use their teeth to grasp and tear, not to chew. Most prey is swallowed whole. Some orca meals can be pretty big. Their stomachs have been found to contain entire seal carcasses.

Orcas live in all the oceans of the world and thus their menu varies. Some populations feed on schooling fish, such as salmon or herring. Others base their diet on larger marine mammals, such as seals or minke whales. Most orcas are opportunistic feeders, taking whatever presents itself with the smallest outlay of energy on the killer whale's part. Normally, orcas spend 75% of their time foraging. They have been known to eat birds, sharks, squid, and porpoises. They may even tackle a blue whale, the largest mammal on earth. At times, orcas travel long distances to feed on a seasonal food supply, but they do not migrate from feeding to breeding grounds the way that gray whales do.

Because orcas are hunters, you might imagine them to be solitary gypsies who prowl and patrol their ocean territories alone. But researchers have made remarkable discoveries about the social organization of killer whales. Thanks to 20 years of field work by these dedicated orca-watchers, we now know that most populations form lifelong family groups. Most research has been carried out in the Pacific Northwest, where relatively stable whale populations have made observation somewhat easier.

The most intimate unit of killer whale society is the maternal group – one female orca and her offspring. They are almost inseparable, staying within a few hundred yards of each other. Orcas bear young every three to ten years. Therefore, calves occasionally nurse for well over a year, and remain exceptionally close to their mothers for up to ten years. Even after the female has had additional calves, killer whales will continue to spend major portions of their lives traveling with their mother.

Once the daughters of a given female are adult and have offspring of their own, they form the next unit of orca life: the subpod. Subpod members invariably travel together and are usually closely related. One or more subpods form a pod, a group that may contain five to 20 individuals. Some pods grow very large – up to 50 whales. Pods tend to travel and hunt together.

As you can see, killer whale life gravitates around the breeding-age females. It seems to be a strongly matriarchal

society, bound together by lifelong ties to the mother. Scientists have yet to identify the father of any specific calf in the wild.

What little is known about orca reproduction is this. Killer whales appear to be polygamous and do not form sexual attachments to just one other whale. Male or bull whales become sexually mature at about 15 years, females or cows at 12-13 years. Breeding can occur throughout the year. In the Pacific Northwest, it is more frequent in late summer and fall. Some cows apparently do not ever bear young. Even after 20 years of field work, scientists have yet to observe killer whale mating activities in the wild.

Once cows become pregnant, the gestation period is 17 months. Generally, they give birth to one calf at a time. Calves are born tail-first, open-eyed and vigorous. Already eight feet at birth, the calf quickly swims to the underside of its mother and finds her hidden nipple. Because cetaceans have no lips and little ability to suck, the mother whale must contract her mammary gland to squirt thick, fat-rich milk into her offspring's mouth.

Sometimes other adult whales assist with the birth or help care for the calf in the important period following the birth. At any given time, only 5% of the whales in a pod are calves, a figure that points up the orca's slow reproduction rate. On the other hand, their mortality rate seems to be equally low.

Awesome: For centuries, natives from Alaska to Peru have hunted the orca and honored its power and mystery in art, song, and story. Killer whales adorn native totem poles, weavings, pottery, magic amulets – even grave markers.

'**K**iller whale mothers are protective of their young, but not overly so. The calves themselves are very curious and playful, especially when they get to be about two years old.

How do I feel when I'm underwater with killer whales? Well, you always know who belongs there and who doesn't. I respect their space and try to make myself as inconspicuous as possible. Of course, the whales have a very clear idea about me from their echolocation sonar. It's a powerful mechanism. When the whales are echolocating, the pulses hit my body with an almost-tangible force.'

— JEFF FOOTT

AS BEFITS its dolphin ancestry, the killer whale has a delightful, almost whimsical sense of play. Majestic in size, the orca nevertheless leaps and cavorts like a mischievous colt. Killer whales have a hydrodynamically perfect body shape and skin type for such acrobatics.

The killer whale repertoire includes breaching. Many whales breach, but few are as spectacular or creative as the orca. Four to ten tons of black-and-white animal shoots as much as 20 feet into the air, falling back onto its belly, side or back at will. Sometimes orcas spiral their bodies during a breach. At others, they flip in mid-air and re-enter the water, nose first. Orcas can even breach horizontally.

Porpoising is another common behavior. The animals alternately swim underwater and on the surface for short distances, just as porpoises do. Orcas also like to tail-lob and flipper-slap, sometimes smacking the water repeatedly with their huge badminton-shaped flippers or their tail flukes. When orcas engage in this behavior, you can see the interesting pattern of black and white on the undersides of their bodies. It may be designed to make the animal appear smaller or less familiar to fish and other prey that may look up and see a killer whale hanging overhead.

Because the pod group is so important to orcas, much of their behavior is synchronized with other pod members. It is beautiful to see orcas resting or sleeping, which they often do in unison. Close enough so their bodies almost touch, the whales dive and blow, moving through the water in a dreamy swimming movement that barely ripples the surface. While resting, orcas

murmur to one another, and their vocalizations get softer and less frequent. Occasionally, the calm is broken by a frisky calf, demanding to be played with, and answered by a scolding cry from its mother.

Killer whales have a 24-hour internal clock, resting and feeding equally during daylight and nighttime hours. Only when they set off to hunt does the unity of the pod break up momentarily. When going after fish, orcas often forage alone. They have also been seen to "herd" salmon together. When pinnipeds or larger animals are hunted, it usually becomes a group effort. Even killer whales do not find it easy to kill adult sea lions or elephant seals. These pinnipeds – which can weigh thousands of pounds – have formidable teeth and strength. Killer whales wear their prey out by repeatedly ramming their victim from below, or by hitting it with their tails until the animal is unconscious or nearly so. Then the orcas pull their victim underwater to drown it.

Orcas use group strategy when going after other whales also. Often, they are not able to kill a full-grown animal. Many whales survive these attacks. You'll see evidence of orca activity in the scars they carry on their bodies.

" When orcas surface to blow, they make a
distinctive sound – a deep whuff!! that carries
a long way. When they tail-lob or fall back
into the water after a leap, the sound is
sharper – more explosive." — JEFF FOOTT

It was – and is – the orca's taste for fish, pinnipeds and other whales that has made them detested by their competitors, the whalers and fishermen."Fat chopper," "sea devil," "a savage sort of Feegee fish"– these were the uncomplimentary names given to killer whales during the 19th and early 20th centuries. Killer whales were also hunted along with other whales, but never with much enthusiasm. For one thing, it took 21 orcas to produce the oil you could get from one sperm whale. For another, orca meat was not tasty by human standards and was used for animal feed. Only Norwegian, Japanese and Russian whalers seemed very interested in orcas. Between 1938 and 1980, they killed over 3,000 of them.

Ordinary humans came to hate and fear killer whales out of ignorance, an emotion pumped up by lurid stories of orca bloodthirstiness. The truth of the matter is that, throughout recorded history, killer whales have had various opportunities to savor human flesh and have never cared for any, thank you. On various occasions, boats or ice floes holding humans have been rammed or bumped by orcas. Other instances have been documented where orcas have approached and examined divers and swimmers. No authenticated report of anyone even being nibbled has ever been filed.

Something wonderful happened in the early 1960s to change mass fear into growing affection. A succession of killer whales were captured and exhibited to the public – the first time this had ever been done. The first two animals died shortly after capture, but the third, a Puget Sound male mistakenly dubbed "Moby Doll," lived about three months. In that short time, Moby Doll became an inadvertent goodwill ambassador for the orca species. The media and an immense outpouring of human curiosity made Moby Doll famous, and the legend of orca ferocity toward man began to die. In 1965, an orca that had gotten tangled in a Canadian fisherman's net was purchased by the Seattle Aquarium. Nicknamed Namu and personally cared for by the Aquarium's owner, the orca lived for a year and was seen by an even bigger audience. The animal's docility and warm response to human contact and coaching showed both biologists and the general public that orcas were not the vicious killers they had been called.

"*On those rare days when the ocean is dead calm, orcas sometimes surface to blow without even breaking the surface tension of the water. It's an amazing display of whale hydrodynamics in action.*"
— JEFF FOOTT

It had now been proven that killer whales could survive in captivity. Not just survive either, but stay healthy enough to cooperate, to learn, and to perform a complex series of behaviors with their trainers. Not surprisingly, many aquaria and aquatic centers began extensive live-capture programs. Between 1965 and 1976, over 100 animals were captured and put on display. The price per orca rose from $8,000 to ten times that amount. It is now reputed to be around one million dollars.

THROUGH these animals on exhibit at places like Sea World, we began to unravel some of the mysteries of orca life. At the same time, concern over the implications of removing whales from the wild population began to surface. As a result, long-range studies of orcas in the wild began. In the past two decades, these studies on behavior, reproduction and population size have greatly increased our understanding. They are uncovering the complex social life of the orca and the communication that binds their lives together.

Aquatic park professionals now know these facts about orca social bonds, and go to incredible lengths to provide substitute nurturing for captive orcas. Each orca has its own human trainer, who forms a special one-on-one relationship with the animal. It is the trainer's voice, touch and daily stimulus that acts as a substitute for pod interaction.

Most of the behaviors that killer whales exhibit in the wild are used for the demonstrations and shows. As trainers point out, orcas often invent the behaviors and stunts and "teach" them to the trainers, not the other way around.

For instance, spyhopping, or taking a visual fix above water, is a common orca behavior. Orcas use their eyes as well as their sonar to locate prey and orient themselves. As they spyhop, orcas sometimes turn slowly in a 360-degree circle. Knowing this, it is easy to see how captive orcas have been persuaded to spin or "dance."

Another orca behavior often put to good use in aquatic shows is synchronized swimming. Soon after birth, wild orcas begin to swim together, diving and surfacing in perfect rhythm. It doesn't take much to encourage them to do it in a tank.

With the help of expert medical attention and caring humans, a few orcas in captivity have lived as long as 20 years to date. Most captive orcas have much briefer lifespans, however. The most recent findings about the mean lifespans of orcas in the wild is 30 years for males, 50 for females.

This poses a dilemma for us, their captors. Do the benefits we derive from orcas on display justify their captivity? There are those who believe we do not have the moral right to remove killer whales from their family pods and almost certainly shorten their life expectancy, just to provide our weekend entertainment, no matter what else is gained. Others point to the great good that has been accomplished by orcas in captivity. Besides providing a wealth of biological data, orcas have become the world's best-known whale ambassadors. The affection they have awakened in the general public has been instrumental in the save-the-whale movement. By seeing Shamu and his kin, people were moved to appreciate not just killer whales but all whales. Thanks to public outcry, many great whales on the verge of extinction in the 1960s and 70s began to receive legislative and other kinds of protection.

'**F**or five weeks I'd been there, set up with my camera on a remote beach in Patagonia on the east coast of Argentina. The first orca attack on the seals was so sudden, so overwhelming, I got buck fever and couldn't remember to press the shutter. It was all over in seconds. But I got additional chances to photograph.*

Patagonian beaches have rocky bottoms, threaded with channels that lead towards the shore. By following the channels, orcas can get near enough to grab prey. The momentum of the attack often brings them right up on the beach, where it takes several waves and a few hops to get back into the ocean.

'

— JEFF FOOTT

"**K**iller whales miss far more often than they succeed in these beach attacks. In fact, they prefer to go after fish in the surf, if it's available."

— JEFF FOOTT

"*Favorite targets? Elephant seal and sea lion pups. Not just because they are less able to defend themselves, but also because the younger animals haven't learned where the killer whales can and cannot approach the shore.*"
— JEFF FOOTT

Ferocity, good luck, strength and wisdom: these are the qualities that native people associated with killer whales. In 200 a.d. Peru, the Nazcan people made line drawings of giant orcas in the stony earth. In California and the Channel Islands, the Chumash Indians revered the orca and carved its smiling image onto magical fetishes.

The richest mythology comes from the Tlingit, Haida and other Indians of the Pacific Northwest and Alaska. To them, the orca – called Skaana or Queet – was sometimes man's rescuer, sometimes a monstrous half-bear, half-whale called the sea-grizzly. A favorite Tlingit character was Gondaquadate, the mythical chief of the orcas. Just a glimpse of him would bring good luck.

Another myth told of Natsihlane, a hunter so good that his wife's jealous brothers decided to do away with him. They took him on a sea lion hunt and left him to die on a rock. The youngest begged the others not to abandon Natsihlane, but to no avail. However, the great hunter was rescued and then carved the first orca from cedar, which came to life and jumped into the sea. Natsihlane directed it to find his brothers-in-law, destroy their canoe, and drown them except for the youngest. After the killer whale did so, Natsihlane told him never to harm humans again.

Like most myths, these stories express underlying truths. Killer whales have indeed proven to be friendly and largely non-aggressive toward humans. The word "largely" has to be inserted, since there have been instances where human trainers have been seriously injured by orcas. In captivity, orcas do get moody. It is thought that the accidents came about mainly because humans were not sensitive enough to the situation.

Killer whales are mysterious enough. But within the orca population of the Pacific Northwest there exists a subgroup (possibly a subspecies) even more mysterious: the transient orcas.

LONG-TERM studies in Puget Sound and British Columbia have revealed that most local orcas belong to geographically defined communities. These animals are called "residents." There proved to be two resident communities in the area. About 180 whales strong, the northern community extends from midway up Vancouver Island to the southeast tip of Alaska. It has 16 known pods. The southern community begins where the northern leaves off, running south into Puget Sound and along the coast of Washington. Three pods – about 80 whales – are in the southern resident community. Resident pods have mutual respect for each other's territories, and will not cross the imaginary boundary line.

The discovery of these home ranges was exciting enough. Then researchers discovered transients – whales that didn't fit the resident mold at all. Transients – of which there may be as many as 100 – are shadowy wanderers, drifting in and out of the resident communities and disappearing altogether for periods of time. Their pods are small – two to seven animals. Sometimes they travel alone. They travel great distances – up to 1,000 miles. And they move quietly. Their vocalizations are few; their dorsal fins tend to be more pointed than the residents; even their diet is different. Transients live on marine mammals; residents, mostly on fish. Transients frequent the small bays and coves, checking out haul-out areas for seal prey.

What do scientists make of these silent gypsies, so different from the gregarious resident whales? Some theorize that transients are marginal animals, excluded for some reason from the main genetic pool. To date, we don't know if resident and transient groups exist in other parts of the world. Some of the studies currently underway may shed more light.

One That Got Away: Scars on a gray whale's tail indicate an orca attack. Killer whales usually hunt together when stalking larger animals such as sea lions or whales. Clearly, they are not successful all of the time. Even when hunting, orcas have a playful nature. Both adult and juvenile whales have been seen toying with their food. For instance, sometimes they hold a salmon in their mouths and pop it in and out many times before dining.

"There is a very gentle, sensitive side to killer whales. You see it in the way they deal with each other and care for each other. And you feel it in their playful, tolerant, sometimes affectionate behavior towards us, their observers and captors."

— JEFF FOOTT

Although many facets of orca life remain a mystery, one thing is clear. Killer whales have a sense of humor or playfulness that has been observed many times. One anecdote comes to us from Juan Carlos López, longtime researcher of Argentine orcas. It was his habit to take a daily walk with his family along a certain beach. One afternoon, a killer whale family showed up and began to swim parallel with the human family as they strolled. Not only did the orcas swim at the same speed, they stopped and started when the López family did. It became a game. The López family experimented in various ways. They walked in a line, they walked abreast, they exchanged positions left and right. The orcas meticulously followed suit. Finally, after any number of changeabouts, the male orca gave several emphatic tail-lobs with his flukes as if to say, "That's enough of this tomfoolery!" and the entire family swam off.

Sometimes killer whale "play" can be traumatic. López also saw an orca pluck a sea lion from the beach, carry it to his killer whale family, play with the luckless animal for 45 minutes, then return it to its original spot. Unharmed physically, the sea lion seemed to have suffered emotionally. From then on, instead of the normal pinniped response of retreating into the water at any sign of danger, the sea lion would hide himself in the bushes well up on shore.

Playthings: Orcas, especially juvenile whales, love to play with kelp, food, and each other. By their teens, killer whales are covered with scratches from years of boisterous bumping, charging, and chasing.

"**W**ithin the waters off Alaska, British Columbia, and Washington, boats and humans often find themselves in the killer whales' environment. Sometimes by accident. With their underwater sonar, these orcas knew all about the boat before they surfaced. On the other hand, the folks in the boat were surprised and a little intimidated at first. It's quite a rush to see animals of that size and majesty come up to greet you."

— JEFF FOOTT

Mystery Spot: Orcas have "core areas" or favorite locales. In British Columbia, the rubbing beach at Robson Bight is one. There, killer whales are drawn to rub their bodies along the small stones of the shallows. Are they grooming? Socializing? Playing? Is it a prelude to mating or birth? The answers are unknown. As the sign indicates, Robson Bight has been declared a marine ecological reserve.

Orcas spend three-quarters of their lives foraging. That still leaves 25% of their time for play, rest, socializing, and travel. Sometimes in their travels, a pod may spontaneously pick up speed until they are traveling as much as 30 mph. This short burst of energy – called speed swimming – may serve to break the monotony. How do the very young orcas keep up? They often ride just behind the mother's dorsal fin, "surfing" the wave off her back. Speed swimming may help in hunting, too. Near the Poles, orcas will speed swim towards a seal-populated iceberg. Just before diving under it, they flip their fins or flukes forward, sending a wave across the iceberg that sometimes washes their prey into the water.

After feeding, some orca populations travel to certain "core areas" to socialize. The area we know most about is Robson Bight in British Columbia. Orcas come here, sometimes on a daily basis, to rub their backs and sides on the smooth stones of the shallows. Only the resident orcas of the northern community gather at Robson. The southern resident orcas favor Haro Strait as their core area.

It is believed that killer whales have other favorite locales in which they gather from time to time. These groupings, called superpods, present a remarkable sight. Observers have seen superpods containing as many as several hundred animals at one time.

"**P**ossibly the most exhilarating thing I've ever seen is the way orcas move in unison. Sometimes a pod will get to a certain geographic point – a headland, for instance – and begin speed swimming or breaching together in what looks like a mini-celebration."
　　　　　　　　　　　　　　　　—JEFF FOOTT

THAT killer whales communicate has been known for some time. Through acoustic studies pioneered by Dr. John Ford (pictured) and others, we are learning the astonishing range and extent of killer whale "language." The animals use two forms of communication: echolocation (a form of sonar) and vocalization. When orcas navigate or search for food, they echolocate, sending out a stream of short, high-energy clicks or pulses. When vocalizing, orcas use whistles, squeaks, high and low tones. These sounds have been grouped into variable and discrete calls. Variable calls differ each time and seem to occur when socializing. Discrete calls sound the same each time. Each pod of whales has 5 to 15 discrete calls that make up its own "dialect." Dialects are so distinctive that individual whales – even aquarium specimens – have been traced to their original pods. Dialects are passed down to succeeding generations also. Studies to date show that the calls remain the same for many generations.

No one claims to know just what the killer whales are "saying" to each other. They may communicate as a way to keep the social organization of the pod tightly knit, or possibly to teach, to warn, to convey emotion.

The Pacific Northwest is probably the only area in the world where it is practical to study orca communications. In that area, 350 to 400 animals have been individually identified, and many of their sounds have been recorded and described. Except for Antarctica, where the largest concentrations of orcas are found, killer whales are thinly scattered throughout

the rest of the oceans of the world. There are also small populations off Iceland, Norway, Alaska, Baja California, Argentina, and Japan. Killer whales are often sighted around Hawaii, the Caribbean, and the Bahamas, and less frequently off the British Isles and in the Mediterranean. Some orcas have even found their way into fresh-water habitats.

Although international legislation regarding orcas has yet to be enacted, the survival of killer whales as a species seems assured. For this we have Moby Doll, Shamu, Orky, Queet, and the rest of the captive orcas to thank. Through them, we have moved from ignorant fear to informed affection for an animal whose powers and abilities are only now being explored to their fullest.

Fun By The Ton: Around 400 pounds at birth, males can reach 10 tons, females 4 to 6. Despite their size, orcas embody grace. Sub-shaped bodies let them breach or leap out of the water both vertically and horizontally.

Special Thanks & Acknowledgments

This book is the natural follow-up to a one-hour film on orcas which Jeff Foott shot for British and U.S. television. An accomplished cinematographer and wildlife photographer, Jeff is also a diver, mountain climber, and skier. To capture his often-elusive subjects, Jeff draws on all these skills and more. The 35 photos you see on these pages represent years of patient observation. Most have never been published before.

Jeff's work has appeared in more than 90 books, magazines, and calendars for *National Geographic, Audubon Society, Sierra Club, Reader's Digest, World Wildlife Fund, Hallmark, Time/Life, Newsweek,* and others. His films cover subjects as diverse as sea otters, elk, Bighorn sheep, manatees, and whooping cranes. Recipient of the Cine Golden Eagle award for his work, Jeff was also nominated for an Emmy for his killer whale film.

A biology major at San Jose State University, Jeff went on to study sea otters at Moss Landing Marine Lab. He is a native Californian who has put down roots in Wyoming, close to some of the wildlife he admires and photographs so eloquently.

A Special Thanks to the following:
Ken Balcomb; Alan Baldridge and the Hopkins Marine Station of Stanford University; Dr. Michael Biggs; the Center for Whale Research at Friday Harbor, Washington; Graeme Ellis; Dr. John Ford; Juan Carlos López; Stubbs Island Charters; Sealand of the Pacific in Victoria, B.C.; Vancouver Aquarium in Vancouver, B.C.

For Further Information

To see orcas in the wild:
• Numerous cruise ships, charter boats, kayak charters, and other vessels operate whale-watching trips in the Puget Sound-British Columbia area. Haro Strait, Johnstone Strait, Robson Bight and Lime Kiln Park on San Juan Island are the areas where killer whales are most often seen. In Washington, most charter vessels operate out of Seattle and Friday Harbor on San Juan Island. In Canada, most charters run out of Vancouver and Victoria, British Columbia.
• Highly recommended are the daily "see-orcas-or-your-money-back" trips run by Stubbs Island Charters, Box 7, Telegraph Cove, British Columbia V0N 3J0. Phone: (604) 928-3185.

To see orcas in marine parks:
A partial list of aquatic parks and oceanaria where orcas may be seen, and in some cases, touched:
Marineland in Niagara Falls, Ontario, Canada
Marine World Africa USA in Vallejo, California
Miami Seaquarium in Miami, Florida
Sealand of the Pacific in Victoria, B.C., Canada
Sea World (parks in California, Florida, Ohio and Texas)
Vancouver Aquarium in Vancouver, B.C., Canada
• Orcas are also on display in oceanaria around the world, including parks in Japan, Argentina, France, Mexico, and other countries.

For further reading:
• *Killer Whales* by Biggs, Ellis, Ford and Balcomb (Phantom Press, 1987)
• *The Whale Called Killer* by Erich Hoyt (Dutton, 1981)
• *The Whale Museum*, P.O. Box 945, Friday Harbor, Washington 98250, (206) 378-4710: non-profit group with newsletter, gift catalog, Adopt-an-Orca program, wildlife cruises, workshops, whale camps for kids, and more.
• *Center for Environmental Education*, 1725 DeSales Street, N.W., Washington, D.C. 20036: non-profit group with newsletter, *Whale Gifts* catalog, environmental book publications, workshops, political advocacy for marine animals.